WOLF SPIDER
(CARRIES ITS BABIES AROUND ON ITS ABDOMEN)

BIRD-DUNG CRAB SPIDER
(HIDES IN PLAIN SIGHT BY LOOKING LIKE BIRD POOP)
(YUCK!)

HAPPY FACE SPIDER
(HAS A HAPPY FACE PATTERN ON ITS BACK—SO CUTE!)

St. ANDREW'S CROSS SPIDER
(RESTS IN THE SHAPE OF AN "X")

PATU DIGUA SPIDER
(WORLD'S SMALLEST SPIDER!)

I'M TRYING TO LOVE SPIDERS.

(It isn't easy.)

ewww...

yuck

GROSS

creepy

weird

WORDS & PICTURES by bethany bARTon

VIKING

An Imprint of Penguin Group (USA)

I KEEP tELLING MYSELF:
"SPIderS ARe COOL."

I WANT to LOVE THEM.

Me
+
SPIderS
4eVA

I MEAN, SPIDERS HAVE BEEN AROUND FOR MILLIONS OF YEARS.

MOVING SILENTLY.
SWINGING INTO ACTION.

SPIDER & DINOSAUR
SPRING BREAK 165 MILLION B.C.

I WANT TO THINK OF THEM LIKE BUG NINJAS...

THAT DIDN'T WORK OUT.

BUT NEXT TIME WILL BE BETTER.

NEXT TIME I'LL FOCUS ON ALL THE COOL SUPERPOWERS SPIDERS HAVE.

LIKE 8 eyes.

EXTREME CLOSE-UP!

AND SPIDERWEBS!

SPIDERWEBS ARE COOL.

FUNNEL WEB →

SHEET WEB →

↑ SPIRAL ORB WEB

SPIDERS SPIN WEBS OUT OF PROTEIN-PACKED SPIDER SILK THEY MAKE THEMSELVES!

THAT'S LIKE YOU OR ME
BUILDING A HOUSE
WITH OUR HAIR

AND THEN
CATCHING
FOOD ON IT.

SOME SPIDERS EVEN HAVE BILLIONS OF TINY HAIRS (CALLED SCOPULAE) ON THEIR LEGS THAT LET THEM STICK ON WALLS OR CEILINGS OR...

OH MY GOSH! THERE'S A SPIDER STUCK ON THERE! SMASH IT! SQUISH IT! GET IT RIGHT NOW!

(WE'RE NOT VERY GOOD AT
LOVING SPIDERS JUST YET.)

INSTEAD THEIR CLOSEST RELATIVES ARE ALSO TOTALLY GROSS.

↗
SCORPION

ARACHNID
FAMILY REUNION

← TICK

BUT IT'S NOT LIKE I'M SCARED OF EVERY ICKY THING.
It's JUST SOMETHING ABOUT SPIDERS!

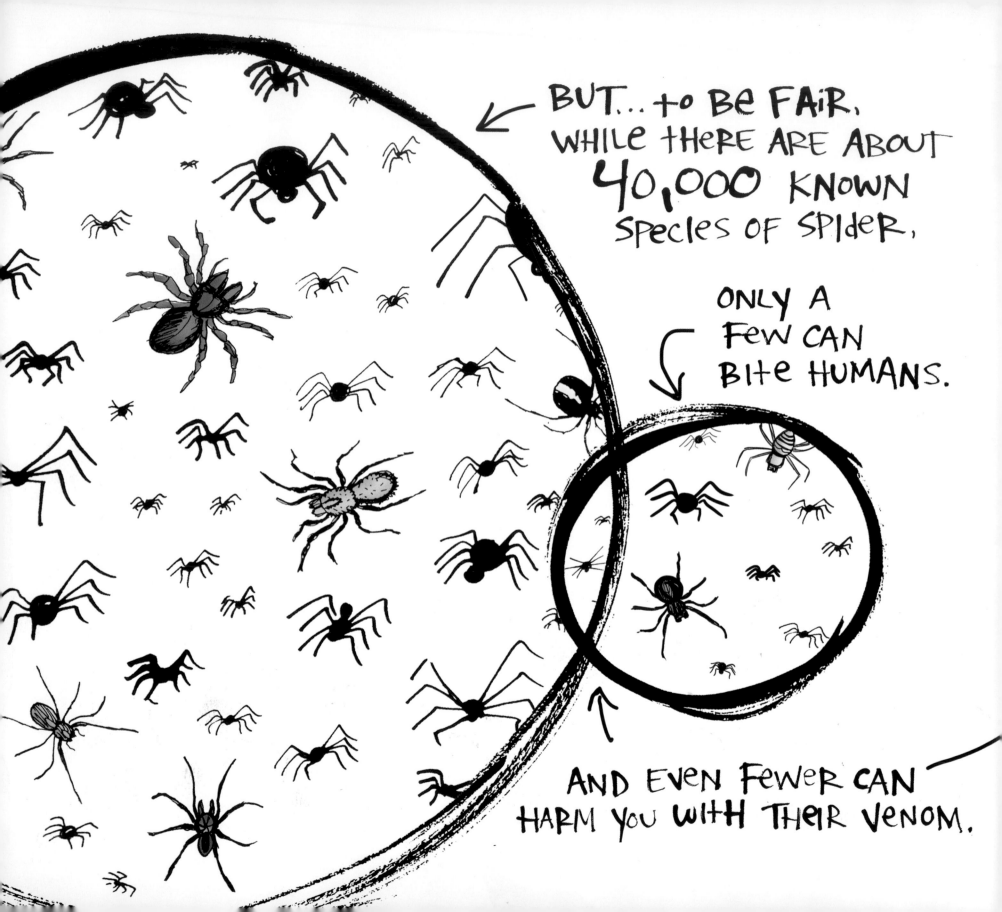

FATAL SPIDER BITES ARE <u>SO</u> RARE,
YOU HAVE A BETTER CHANCE OF
GETTING STRUCK BY LIGHTNING!

you.

OH. MY. GOSH.

OKAY, DON'T PANIC...
BUT THERE IS DEFINITELY
A SPIDER OVER THERE.

AND WE'RE NOT
GONNA SQUISH IT
THIS TIME, RIGHT?

WE'LL JUST TRY TO... PET HIM...? MAYBE?

CAN YOU PET SPIDERS?

Let's TRY!

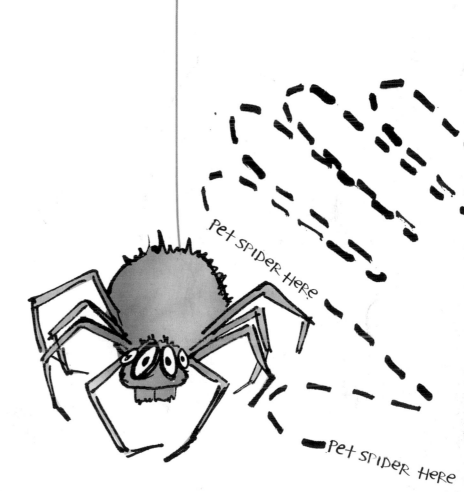

WHOOPS! NOPE.

WE SQUISHED HIM.

LIKE EATING BUGS!

THAT'S GOTTA BE HELPFUL, RIGHT?

A SINGLE SPIDER CAN EAT OVER 75 POUNDS OF BUGS IN A YEAR!

75 lb.
OF
BUGS
(TOTAL GROSSNESS)

75 lb.
OF
DOG
(A FULL-GROWN BOXER)

I've even HEARD THAT some FARMERS use SPIDERS to keep HARMFUL INSECTS out of THEIR CROPS.

AND — OH WAIT...
LOOKS LIKE SOME OF THOSE
BUGS MADE IT OVER HERE...

GET OUT
OF HERE, BUGS!
I CAN'T EVEN READ MY BOOK
WITH ALL THESE...

HEY,
WHAT'S THAT
SPIDER
DOING?

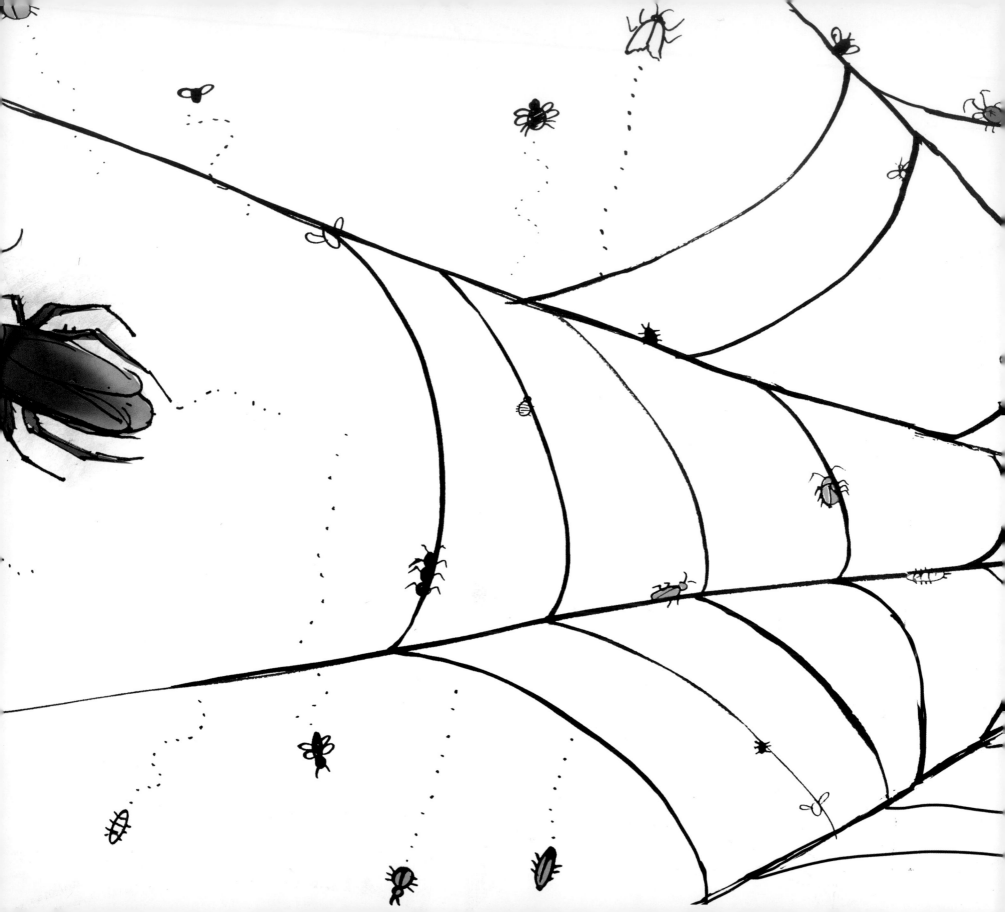

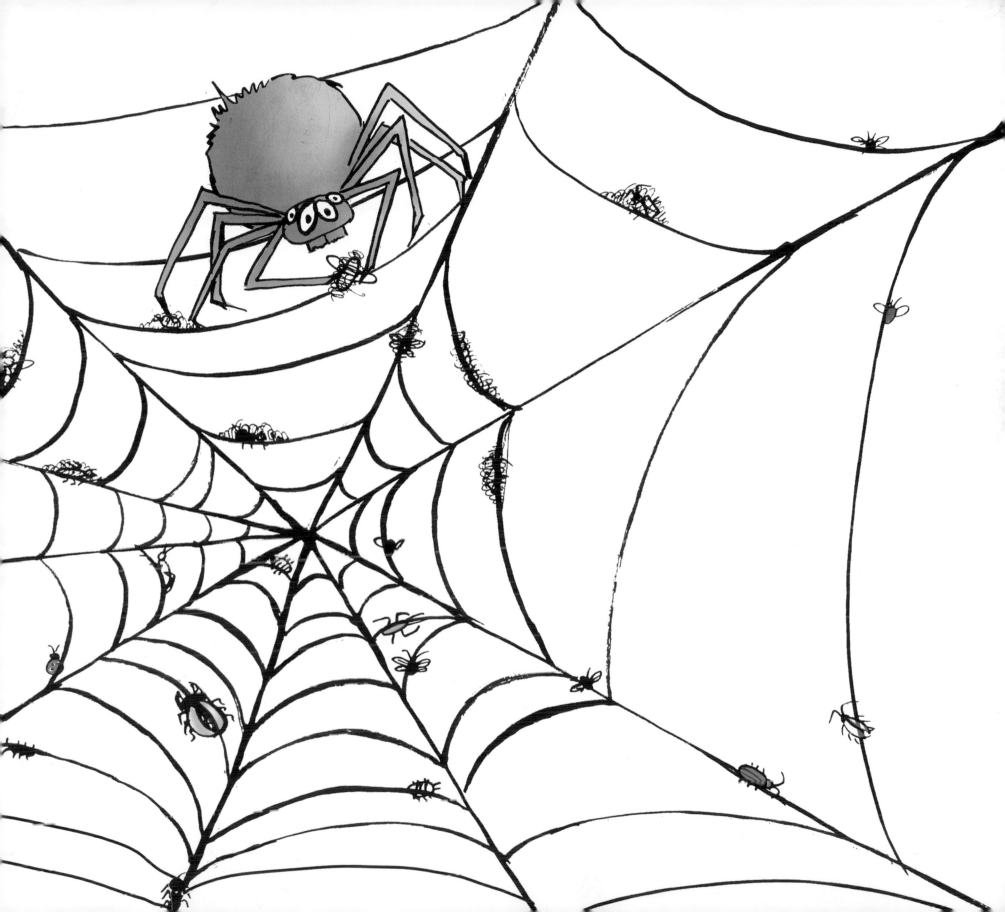

WOW! THANKS, LITTLE GUY! THAT WAS REALLY IMPRESSIVE!

(SPIDER PRESENTS ← FOR YOU.)

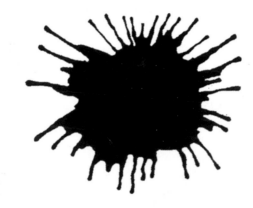

(ONE THING AT A TIME.)

For Leo: The Buddy, The Beastie, My Little Monster

(With a side order of extra thanks to Cindy Barton,
for watching him so I could draw all these spiders.)

VIKING
Published by the Penguin Group
Penguin Group (USA) LLC
375 Hudson Street
New York, New York 10014

USA * Canada * UK * Ireland * Australia
New Zealand * India * South Africa * China

penguin.com
A Penguin Random House Company

First published in the United States of America by Viking, an imprint of Penguin Young Readers Group, 2015

LIBRARY OF CONGRESS CATALOGING-IN-PUBLICATION DATA
Barton, Bethany, date- author, illustrator.
I'm trying to love spiders / written and illustrated by Bethany Barton.
pages cm
Summary: "This fresh and very funny non-fiction picture book shares lots of fascinating facts about spiders
in an entirely captivating way. If I'm Trying to Love Spiders doesn't cure your spider phobia, it'll at least make
you appreciate how amazing they are . . . and laugh a lot as you learn about them."—Provided by publisher.
Audience: Ages 4–8.
Audience: K to grade 3.
ISBN 978-0-670-01693-8 (hardcover)
1. Spiders—Juvenile literature. I. Title. II. Title: I am trying to love spiders.
QL458.4.B365 2015   595.4'4—dc23   2014031680

Manufactured in China

7   9   10   8

The artwork for this book was rendered using inks, paper, computers, and concentrated awesome.
Almost no spiders were harmed in the making of this book.

DIVING BELL SPIDER
(STORES AIR IN UNDERWATER WEBS SO IT CAN LIVE ALMOST ENTIRELY UNDERWATER!)

GOLDEN WHEEL SPIDER
(FLIPS ON ITS SIDE AND "CARTWHEELS" DOWN THE SAND DUNES TO ESCAPE PREDATORS)

ASSASSIN SPIDER
(PREYS ONLY ON OTHER SPIDERS!)

WRITING SPIDER
(DRAWS A ZIGZAG PATTERN IN ITS WEB WITH SILK)